A Bird

in Trouble

empower

publishing

A Bird
in Trouble

by

Dianne Nicholas Goodrich

Empower Publishing

Winston-Salem

empower

publishing

Empower Books
PO Box 26701
Winston-Salem, NC 27114

First Empower Books edition published
April, 2021
Empower Books, Feather Pen, and all production design are trademarks of Indigo Sea Press, used under license.

For information regarding bulk purchases of this book, digital purchase and special discounts, please contact the publisher at empoweryourpublishing.com

Dianne Nicholas Goodrich, Author
Anna McCullough, Illustrator
Dr. Linda Fox Felker, Editor, President of Felker Consulting, Inc., Winston-Salem, North Carolina.
Pan Morelli, Cover Design

Manufactured in the United States America
ISBN 978-1-63066-517-3

This book is dedicated to our daughter Mary Beth, her husband, Zac, and our two grandchildren, Waylon and Keeley.

This is a true story about a bird in trouble. The names have been changed but isn't it wonderful that God never does!

—Dianne Nicholas Goodrich

It was a beautiful, sunny, early Friday evening when a most unusual thing happened at the McMaster's house.

Mary and her daughter were taking their dog, Heidi, outside for a potty break.

Her husband and son were outside to put up a tent for their father-son outing. They looked forward to sleeping under the stars that night.

A friend of Mary's daughter came over to play. They ran to the backyard to enjoy time in the playhouse that PawPaw built for his grandchildren.

"Well, I am elected to take Heidi to the bathroom myself," Mary said to herself.

As Mary walked Heidi to her perfect spot, she saw a tree with a clear view of a bird that was caught in a branch shaped like a "V".

Mary was astonished the bird did not try to fly away as she came near.

"Oh No! Is this bird hurt?" she thought. She held tight to Heidi's leash, and moved closer to the bird. She noticed how this poor bird could not move in this V-shaped branch.

Mary knew she needed to help this bird. After Heidi went to the potty, she took the dog inside and went back to the bird.

Mary put the bird's feet in the palm of her hand and pushed up. She felt insecure and wondered if the bird would try to peck her.

Mary had always heard that mockingbirds were aggressive. She gave it a try and used her hand to push the bird up, but it did not work.

"Okay, I can't do this. I need help." Mary called to her husband for help, but he did not hear her. Mary whispered a short prayer and tried again.

She slowly pushed the bird up, and this time, the bird was loose. The bird started to fly away, but only made it to the ground and sat there puzzled.

Then, the bird gathered her strength and flew away.

Mary was satisfied that she helped this bird.

As she watched the bird fly away, she thought of God's word about faithfulness and confidence.

1 Timothy 1:12 tells us that the Lord Jesus enables us to be counted faithful to whatever He has for us to do.

Philippians 4:13 tells us that the strength to do what God calls us to do comes from him.

That bird might have died if Mary had decided to give up.

But with God's help, she was faithful and confident, and was able to rescue the bird in trouble.

A day or two later, Mary went outside in her yard and started pulling weeds from her beauty spot.

To her amazement, she noticed a bird nest in a bush with three baby mockingbirds.

Her thoughts went back to the bird she rescued a few days before. She pondered a question to herself.

Could the bird she rescued be the mama bird to these little ones? She was happy that she had been a faithful and confident servant.

www.ingramcontent.com/pod-product-compliance
Lightning Source LLC
LaVergne TN
LVHW072112070426
835509LV00003B/130